Take a Giant Leap, Neil Armstrong!

by Peter and Connie Roop

SCHOLASTIC INC.

New York   Toronto   London   Auckland   Sydney
Mexico City   New Delhi   Hong Kong   Buenos Aires

For Sterling, as he takes giant steps
toward his dreams!

ISBN 0-439-67626-6

36 35 34 33 32 31 30   18 19 20 21 22 23 24

Printed in the U.S.A.   40
First printing, March 2005

Contents

Introduction

Neil Armstrong made history when he became the first person to set foot on the moon. Do you know that Neil's trip to the moon was his last space trip as an astronaut?

Neil Armstrong and his fellow astronaut Buzz Aldrin were the first people to land on the moon. Do you know that going to the moon had been Neil Armstrong's dream since high school?

Neil Armstrong's family moved many times. Do you know that Neil lived in sixteen different places in Ohio when he was growing up?

Neil Armstrong read ninety books in first grade. Do you know that Neil was such a good reader he skipped half of second grade?

Neil Armstrong loved to fly airplanes. Do you know that Neil earned his airplane pilot's license before he earned his license to drive a car?

Neil Armstrong loved to fly real airplanes as a teenager and as an adult. Do you know that Neil built dozens of model airplanes by hand, without kits, when he was growing up?

Neil Armstrong was an excellent airplane pilot who could fly planes in loops. Do you know that when Neil was young, he often got carsick?

Neil Armstrong was a hard worker all his life. Do you know that Neil had jobs in a cemetery, a bakery, and a grocery store when he was young?

Neil Armstrong made history by being the first person to walk on the moon. Do you know that Neil hopes people will walk on Mars one day?

The answers to these questions lie in who Neil Armstrong was as a young person. This book is about Neil Armstrong before he made history.

1

Neil Armstrong Is Born

Tuesday, August 5, 1930, was a hot, humid day on Will and Caroline Korspeter's farm in northwestern Ohio. Tall green corn rustled in the fields. Cows drank cool water from the trough. Chickens pecked for food in the dirt. Hogs grunted as they soaked up the summer sun. Maggie, the Korspeters' pony, nibbled grass.

People in the nearby town of Wapakoneta went about their daily business. Many of them were relatives of the Korspeter family. Tuesday was just another summer day in this hardworking farming community.

Inside the Korspeters' farmhouse the day was far from normal. The Korspeters' daughter, Viola Armstrong, was just about to have her first baby.

Viola, her mother, Caroline, and her grandmother had all been born in the Korspeters' two-story wooden house. The house was almost one hundred years old. Viola's great-grandparents built the farmhouse when they settled in Ohio, around 1850. Viola Armstrong was excited and pleased that her baby would be born in her family's home.

Grandma Korspeter boiled water. She had to be ready when the baby was born. There was no doctor near the Korspeters' farm. Grandma would have to deliver the baby all by herself. This was not a problem for Grandma Korspeter. She had delivered many other babies. She knew what she was doing. Grandma was ready with hot water and helping hands when Viola called her from her bed.

Grandpa Korspeter checked on his daughter as he did his farm chores. He wished they had a telephone. But the nearest phone was miles away on another farm. Grandpa Korspeter wanted to call his son-in-law, Stephen

Armstrong, to tell him the baby was on its way. But Mr. Armstrong was working in another town. They would just have to wait for Mr. Armstrong to come home. They hoped he would arrive before the baby did!

That afternoon, with her mother's help, Viola Armstrong had her baby. It was a boy! As Viola held her newborn son, she was more eager than ever for her husband to hurry home. She wanted him to share this special moment, too.

Grandma cleaned the baby. She wrapped him in a blanket. Grandma turned on the radio and began making dinner. As she worked, Grandma hummed along to a new song on the radio. The song was "Where Have You Been?" Grandma Korspeter certainly had no idea where her grandson would be going one day!

Grandpa Korspeter smiled as he finished his farm chores. He was proud to have a grandson. Grandpa was looking forward to teaching his grandson all about farming. He would teach his grandson how to ride Maggie, their pony. He would teach the boy how

to care for the farm animals. He would show him how to pitch hay.

Grandpa Korspeter knew it took a lot of hard work to run a successful farm. But still, he hoped that maybe his grandson would grow up to be a farmer, too. Grandpa had no idea that instead of one day riding a tractor on a farm, his grandson would be riding a rocket into space!

A cloud of dust rose from the road running in front of the farm. A car sped up the driveway. Stephen Armstrong jumped out of the car and ran into the house. He stopped in the doorway for a moment to catch his breath. Then Grandma Korspeter placed a little bundle in Stephen's arms. Mr. Armstrong gazed into his son's bright blue eyes for the first time.

Viola and Stephen named their son Neil Alden Armstrong.

The Armstrongs admired Neil from his head to his feet. No one in that Ohio farmhouse could have guessed that one day those two feet would be the first ever to walk on the moon.

2
Neil's Early Years

Neil's father worked for the state of Ohio. His job was to make sure that every county accurately kept track of its tax money. He checked to see how the money was being spent. Mr. Armstrong's job meant that he had to drive to many towns and cities in Ohio. While he was gone on trips, baby Neil and his mother lived with Neil's grandparents.

In 1930, when Neil was born, many people in the United States were suffering. Jobs were very hard to find. Thousands of families moved from place to place looking for work, food, and a place to live. This time was called the Great Depression.

Neil's family was fortunate. Mr. Armstrong had a good job. Neil's grandparents owned their farm. They grew most of the food they needed. They loved having Neil and his mother living with them.

More than one hundred of Neil's aunts, uncles, and cousins lived nearby in Wapakoneta or on their own farms in the surrounding countryside. They were farmers, teachers, judges, politicians, and businessmen. Years later, when Neil returned from the moon, the people of Wapakoneta had a big celebration for him. Neil smiled and shyly greeted them by saying, "I guess I'm related to most of you."

Neil's mother's relatives had come to Ohio from Germany. Her grandfather Frederick Koenig had sailed to America in the mid-nineteenth century. Frederick carved his farm out of the Ohio wilderness, the same farm where Neil Armstrong would be born one day.

Neil's father's relatives, the Armstrongs, came to Ohio from Scotland in the 1700s. His great-great-grandfather Captain John Armstrong was a farmer, merchant, and soldier.

Captain Armstrong built his home near a Native American village called Wapakoneta.

Neil had many enriching experiences while living on his Korspeter grandparents' farm. Soon after Neil learned how to walk, his grandfather taught him how to ride Maggie. Neil watched his grandfather feed hay to the cattle. He saw him milk the cows. He watched Grandpa throw scraps to the hungry hogs.

Neil enjoyed being with his mother and grandmother, too, as they did their jobs. They had to wash and iron everyone's clothes. They had a garden to plant, weed, and harvest. There were cucumbers to pickle. There were blackberries and raspberries to pick, cook, and make into delicious jams. Bread had to be baked and meals cooked.

Neil knew his father took his job very seriously. He made sure every penny of taxes was accounted for. But Neil missed his father when he was away.

When Neil was two years old, his parents took him to see his first airplanes. They drove

over bumpy country roads to Cleveland, Ohio, to see the National Air Races.

Neil often felt sick from the motion in the car. Sometimes his father could only drive twenty minutes before he had to stop so Neil wouldn't get sick. Then, when Neil felt better, the trip would continue.

That day Neil didn't mind being in the car. They were going to see airplanes!

At the airfield Neil enjoyed the roaring engines and spinning propellers. Neil watched in wonder as airplanes zoomed overhead doing flying tricks. He gazed at the speeding airplanes racing in the sky. Neil stared at the many different kinds of planes taking off and landing.

Neil's first encounter with flying made quite an impression. His mother said, "He was so fascinated, he was never ready to leave." When his parents said it was time to go, Neil begged, "One more. One more!" Knowing how much Neil liked the airplanes, his parents took him back to the Cleveland Airport as often as they could.

3
Neil Flies for the First Time

When Neil was three years old his sister, June, was born. Then, a year and a half later, his brother, Dean, was born. Mrs. Armstrong had her hands full caring for three children. Neil was disappointed they couldn't go to see the airplanes as often. But he did enjoy having a little sister and brother to play with.

In 1936, when Neil was six years old, the Armstrongs were living in Warren, Ohio. One Sunday morning Neil and his father had an amazing adventure. They were on their way to Sunday school. At the local airfield they saw a special airplane.

This airplane had three big motors with huge propellers. One motor was on the nose

of the airplane. Each wing had a motor, too. The plane was called a Ford TriMotor.

The TriMotor was unusual because it was made out of sheet metal. Most airplanes in 1936 were built out of wood and canvas. The Ford TriMotor airplane was nicknamed the *Tin Goose*, and it was big enough to carry thirty passengers!

Neil's father knew the *Tin Goose* was taking people up for rides. He also knew how much his son was fascinated by airplanes. Remembering that day, Mr. Armstrong said, "The earlier in the day that you flew, the cheaper it was, so we didn't get to Sunday school that day. We took a plane ride."

Neil hopped out of the car and dashed over to the *Tin Goose*. He ran his hands over the metal sides of the airplane. Neil and his father joined the line of people waiting their turn to fly in the *Tin Goose*. Neil watched other boys with their fathers climb into the plane. Every once in a while one of the dads would look into the plane, shake his head,

and decide not to fly. Neil saw the disappointment on those boys' faces.

Finally, the Armstrongs' turn came. Neil stepped through the door. His father followed him. Neil sat down and buckled his seat belt. Seat belts were new in airplanes. But Neil had read about them in *Air Trails* magazine so he knew how seat belts worked. Neil showed his father how to buckle the seat belt.

Mr. Armstrong was a little frightened. He worried that taking Neil up into the air might not be such a good idea after all. But Neil was not scared. He looked out his window. He watched an engine sputter to life. Slowly, the propeller began spinning. It spun faster and faster until it was just a blur. The other two engines roared and began spinning their propellers. Neil was staring so hard at the propeller that he didn't notice some of the other passengers closing their eyes because they were so scared.

Suddenly, the *Tin Goose* began moving. It bumped down the grassy airfield, gaining speed little by little. Then, all at once, the airplane lifted off the ground.

For the first time in his life, Neil Armstrong was flying!

Neil gazed out the window. He saw the people below getting smaller and smaller. Farmhouses and barns looked like toys. Farm fields lay below Neil like a giant patchwork quilt. Ponds and lakes seemed like puddles.

The bouncing plane made Neil feel sick to his stomach. Neil ignored it. There was too much to see and enjoy to have motion sickness!

Neil's father hadn't yet dared to look out the window. Finally, Mr. Armstrong peeked past Neil. He knew people would ask him what he had seen from high in the sky. He looked, then quickly looked away. Flying was not for Stephen Armstrong!

Neil Armstrong, however, scarcely blinked his eyes. He didn't want to miss a thing.

All at once, the plane turned hard to the left. The *Tin Goose* began dropping back down to Earth. Behind Neil someone screamed.

Some fathers, thinking they were going to crash, grabbed their sons. Neil, instead, was disappointed. He had only been in the air for fifteen minutes. He wanted to fly forever!

The *Tin Goose* touched down and rolled to a stop. Neil reluctantly unbuckled his seat belt and climbed out. Neil turned around and looked at the plane. Mr. Armstrong climbed out behind Neil. His legs were shaking. Mr. Armstrong walked straight to his car. He didn't even glance back at the *Tin Goose*.

The moment they walked through the door at home, Mrs. Armstrong knew that Neil and his father had done something special. Mrs. Armstrong said, "Dad especially looked so guilty, but Neil clearly loved it. He was really impressed, and I think his love for flying started that day."

4
Planes and More Planes

After that first flight, Neil's fascination with airplanes soared. Neil began to learn all he could about airplanes.

Neil's mother was eager for her children to learn new things, too. She shared magazines with them. She read books to them. Neil enjoyed books so much that he knew how to read before he went to first grade.

Neil's mother loved music. She passed this love on to Neil. Neil learned to read music and play the piano. He enjoyed playing duets with his mother. Later, when Neil was an astronaut, he often played the piano to entertain his friends and family.

Neil liked music so much that he would sneak downstairs at six in the morning and turn on the radio. His favorite show was *Hank Keene's Gang*. Neil especially liked the show's songs. He played the radio softly so he wouldn't disturb his family.

Mr. Armstrong's job kept the family moving. Sometimes they lived in houses; other times, they stayed in apartments. To make moving easier, the Armstrongs didn't own any furniture. They lived in places that were already furnished. Each time they moved, the Armstrongs packed their personal belongings, hopped into the car, and drove off to a new place. When Mr. Armstrong finished his work, they moved again. By the time Neil was twelve years old, his family had lived in fifteen different places!

When he was six years old, Neil went to first grade. He liked school, especially math and science. Neil read a lot in the first and second grades. In first grade Neil read ninety books all by himself. He read so many books that he was able to skip the last half of second grade and go straight into third grade.

By the end of the year Neil was reading books for fifth-graders!

Neil began reading books and magazines about airplanes and flying. He read the science fiction books of Jules Verne and H. G. Wells in which people travel in space, even to the moon!

Neil became especially excited to learn about two famous men from his home state of Ohio, Wilbur and Orville Wright. Through determined thinking, experimenting, and problem solving, the Wright brothers built, and flew, the first airplane.

Neil decided to build his own airplanes. He would build model airplanes. Neil wanted to understand just how each piece of an airplane worked. He built his model airplanes by hand, using materials he found at home. Neil knew there were model airplane kits he could buy, but he wanted to make his planes his own way. Neil's first airplanes were simple. He cut wooden bodies and wings. He made spinning propellers. He painted his planes.

As he gained more experience, Neil took on more challenging planes to build. He added more details. He made complicated designs.

Neil built a TriMotor, like the plane he had first flown in. He built a speedy Italian airplane. He even built a model of a German plane that had twelve motors!

Neil hung one, two, then three airplanes from his bedroom ceiling. Neil's mother, seeing her son's enthusiasm for his airplanes, let Neil hang his planes wherever he wanted to. Soon Neil's airplanes began "flying" throughout the house.

Now, whenever it was time for the Armstrongs to move, Neil carefully packed his planes along with his clothes. Before the rest of the family had settled into their new home, Neil's planes were "flying" from the ceilings again!

Neil also built airplanes with friends. Since the Armstrongs moved so often, Neil was always meeting new boys and making new friends. Neil shared what he knew about building model planes with his friends.

Sometimes the boys threw their model planes out of a second-story window just to see them fly. The planes didn't stay up very long, however, and many crashed.

When Neil wasn't reading or building airplanes, he loved to be outside. He joined the Boy Scouts. He learned how to cook over a campfire and put up a tent. He learned how to tie knots. He learned how to use a compass and find his way in the woods. Neil enjoyed camping with his friends.

Neil went fishing and swimming. He joined his mother in songs on the piano. He played games with June and Dean.

Neil enjoyed visiting Grandma and Grandpa Korspeter on their farm. He helped his grandfather with the farm chores. Neil worked hard, but he didn't want to be a farmer. Grandpa Korspeter said Neil "was never really interested in farming." Grandpa would have been proud to know that one day, after he made history, Neil Armstrong would own a dairy farm.

5
Neil Works and Plays Hard

But no matter what else he did, Neil didn't forget about airplanes and flying. He read every airplane magazine he could find. He cut out airplane pictures and made a special scrapbook.

Neil enjoyed doing many things on Earth, but his eye was on the sky. Neil thought about flying so much that he often had the same dream at night. Neil dreamed that he could hold his breath and float up to the clouds. In his dream Neil looked down and saw the world below. This was Neil's favorite dream.

When he was nine years old, Neil was given a special present. His parents knew Neil was fascinated with space so they gave him a telescope. When the night sky was clear, Neil aimed his telescope at space. He stared at stars. He searched for planets. He gazed at the moon. Neil's friend Joey Carter said, "I imagine he was thinking about the day he would fly into space himself."

Neil needed money to buy materials to build more model airplanes. He also needed money to buy more flying magazines. Neil needed a job.

Neil was ten years old when got his first job. He cut grass in the local cemetery and was paid ten cents an hour. Neil worked hard at his job. But he still had time for his friends, the Scouts, and of course, his airplanes.

In seventh grade Neil became very interested in the baritone horn. Neil enjoyed this musical instrument so much that he wanted a horn of his own. And he wanted to take lessons. But a new horn cost seventy-five dollars.

Neil knew his parents had little money to spare. Neil's brother, Dean, said, "In our family if you wanted something, you'd better work. Everybody started working when he was eight or nine years old — and you just never stopped."

Neil needed a better-paying job. He began working in a bakery after school. His job was to clean out the ovens. He also helped to make doughnuts. Each night Neil made 1,320 doughnuts!

When Neil stopped working at the bakery, he took other jobs. But he always made certain he could do the job well, earn his pay fairly, and still have time for his schoolwork, family, and airplanes.

In 1942, when Neil was twelve years old, his family moved to Wapakoneta, Ohio. This was Neil's last move until he went away to college. Now that he was back in Wapakoneta, Neil was happy to be near his grandparents again. He could see them more often and was there to help them.

Neil worked hard in school and after school. He was a substitute paper delivery boy. He worked in a grocery store. He put

things on shelves at a drugstore. Richard Brading, who owned the drugstore, said Neil was "hardworking, never wasted time on reading comic books. But he would jump at the flying magazines when they came in."

Neil even began his own band with three friends. Now he could play his new baritone horn more often. The band was paid sometimes to play for parties. Neil liked the extra money.

At first the band was called The German Band because all the boys had German ancestors. But in 1942 the United States was at war with Germany. The band changed its name to the Mississippi Moonshiners Band. They had a reputation for playing well, but for also playing loud "with a capital L."

Neil was active and liked to be outside. He still participated in scouting. He began working to become an Eagle Scout, the highest rank. There never seemed to be enough hours in a day for all the things Neil Armstrong wanted to do.

6
Neil Studies, Experiments, and Dreams

One day Neil heard that a man named Jacob Zint owned a telescope that was much bigger than Neil's telescope. And he lived on Pearl Street, just a few blocks away from Neil's house!

Neil had to see Mr. Zint's telescope. Maybe Mr. Zint would even let Neil look through it at the stars and moon! Neil's friend Joey said, "I'd never seen him (Neil) so excited. His eyes were on fire." Neil said, "Do you think he'll (Mr. Zint) let us look through it? He just has to. We have to make friends with him."

The next time Joey saw Mr. Zint he told him about Neil Armstrong. He asked if Neil and he might be able to look through his telescope one night. Mr. Zint was very pleased that Neil and Joey were interested in space. Mr. Zint was just as excited about flying and the stars as Neil was.

Mr. Zint told Neil how he made his telescope himself. He made telescope lenses from glass. He put roller-skate wheels on the telescope platform so he could turn it in order to see in a big circle.

Then Mr. Zint aimed his telescope at the sky. Neil eagerly waited his turn to look through the lens. When Neil looked up, he saw a sight that took his breath away: A brilliant meteor shower was flashing through the sky.

Neil Armstrong's feet were firmly planted on Earth, but his heart was in the heavens.

Neil spent every free minute he could with Mr. Zint and his telescope. Mr. Zint taught Neil about the constellations. He showed Neil gas clouds in space that were millions of miles wide. Neil observed the clouds through the sharp lens of the telescope.

Neil and Mr. Zint talked about space

travel. Neil wondered if there was life in outer space. Mr. Zint told him he thought Mars might have life on it. Mr. Zint said that Neil "would get a very intent look whenever he looked through the scope. But I do believe the moon was Neil's point of interest right from the start."

Neil worked even harder at school and at his jobs. His father said, "The boy had a wonderful capacity for doing hard work." His brother, Dean, said, "Neil liked school. Math and science were his favorite subjects."

Neil did very well in math, chemistry, weather, and astronomy. These subjects would help him toward his goal of becoming an airplane pilot.

Neil also kept up with his reading. Neil's goal was to read 101 long books before he turned fourteen years old. Neil carried a notebook in which he kept track of what he had read. Neil read books like *Principles of Flight*, *Modern Flight*, and *The Young American's Aviation Annual*. His brother said, "Neil devoured books." He read about pioneer fliers, especially the Wright brothers. His mother said, "He read everything about them. He thought they were the greatest of men."

One classmate said, "By the time we were in high school, he had read more books than the rest of the class combined." Neil knew whole parts of Shakespeare's plays and the Bible by heart. Before long, Neil passed his goal of 101 books.

Neil learned all he could about radios. He knew they were the key to helping a pilot find his way in the sky. He took apart the family radio so he could understand how it worked. And he put it back together! Neil borrowed and read every book he could find about radios. He added these books to his list.

Neil also did more experiments with airplanes. He knew that the Wright brothers had made some very important discoveries in a wind tunnel they built. Neil decided to build a wind tunnel, too. Neil planned to create a strong wind in his tunnel and test airplane parts.

Neil and Dean collected the things they

needed. They took old stovepipes from a junkyard. They bought an electric motor and switch. They even found an old airplane propeller.

Neil and Dean set up their wind tunnel in their basement. They aimed the tunnel's opening up the basement stairs. Then they turned on the motor. The propeller spun and created a strong wind that blew through the tunnel. Suddenly, the lights went out. The motor stopped. They had blown an electrical fuse. First they fixed the fuse, then Neil sent Dean upstairs to invite their mother to see the wind tunnel.

As Mrs. Armstrong was coming down the basement stairs, Neil switched on the motor. A gigantic blast of air hit Mrs. Armstrong. The force of the wind blew off her coat! And it blew out a basement window.

Dean said, "Neil thought that was the funniest thing he'd ever done — but Mother didn't."

7
Neil Takes Off!

Neil also experimented with a small steam engine that turned a wheel. One of Neil's experiments changed light into electricity. He also built small radios.

One day Neil told his parents about a very special project he was working on. Neil secretly had bought a wrecked airplane. He rebuilt the plane. When Neil finally told his parents about his secret project, the plane was almost ready to fly. Only the engine needed more work.

Neil's parents had been supportive of his plane models and his experiments. But they put an end to his rebuilt-plane project. If Neil was determined to fly, he would have to fly in a real plane and learn from a real pilot.

So that's what Neil made up his mind to do.

There was a small airport near Neil's home in Wapakoneta. The airport was called Port Koneta. It was little more than a large field covered with rye grass. The grass was thick enough for a small plane to land on safely. Sometimes, however, the grass grew so tall that airplane propellers cut the grass as the planes rolled along for takeoff. The grass flew back onto the plane's windshield.

Port Koneta was also a challenging place for small planes to land. The field was windy, especially in winter. At times, planes had to almost glide down to land.

This didn't matter to Neil Armstrong. In fact, such conditions actually helped Neil become a skilled pilot very quickly. He learned how to take off and land in difficult, dangerous situations.

But before he could fly, Neil had to solve one big problem. How was he going to pay for flying lessons? They cost nine dollars an hour. Neil knew he needed many hours of flying practice with an experienced pilot before he could get his own pilot's license.

Neil found the solution. He would work harder at his jobs and save every penny for the flying lessons. Neil made forty cents an hour working. It would take him more than twenty-two hours of work to be able to pay for one hour in the air. But for Neil it was worth it!

His parents agreed to let Neil take flying lessons. They knew how much he wanted to learn how to fly, and they were relieved that he wasn't going to fly in his rebuilt plane!

So one day, when he was fifteen years old, Neil rode his bike out to Port Koneta for his first flying lesson. He had his nine dollars. Neil was too young to have his driver's license, but now it was to time to learn how to fly.

After his first lesson Neil knew he would keep flying until he got his pilot's license. Whenever he had the chance, Neil biked or got a ride out to Port Koneta. Aubrey Knudegard, who owned the flying school, saw Neil's enthusiasm. Mr. Knudegard let Neil stay at

the field when his lessons were over. Neil listened to other pilots. He washed and cleaned airplanes for extra money.

Before long, Neil had mastered flying a small airplane. He learned how to judge the tricky winds and make safe takeoffs and landings. He learned how to use the airplane's compass to help him find his way. He learned how to check his airplane to make sure everything was working correctly. Neil learned the many precautions to make a safe, successful flight.

Neil learned so much, so fast that before the end of the year he was flying solo, without a flight instructor.

Neil's dream of flying had come true. He didn't have to hold his breath in his dreams to soar with the birds. He had mastered the mysteries of an airplane and could now fly one.

On August 5, 1946, his sixteenth birthday, Neil got up very early. He jumped on his bike to head to the Auglaize Flying Field. Today was the day Neil Armstrong would take the test for his pilot's license.

At the airfield Neil reviewed the flying rule book and took the written test. He passed. Neil demonstrated his ability to take off, fly solo, and land safely. He passed this test, too.

That day Neil Armstrong received his pilot's license. Neil proudly showed his license to his parents. Neil might not have a license to drive their car yet, but he could fly an airplane!

Neil was thrilled to be able to fly. But he also knew the dangers of flight. Neil got his flying license in 1946. This was only forty-three years after the Wright brothers had made their first flight. Neil understood how airplanes worked. He also knew that there was still much to learn about airplanes.

8

Neil Learns Some
Difficult Lessons

One sad day, Neil learned the hard way how dangerous flying really was.

Neil was hiking with some friends out near the airport. The boys heard an airplane overhead and looked up. Neil recognized the plane. It was one he had taken lessons in.

Neil realized, however, that something was terribly wrong. The plane was flying too fast and too low to land safely. Neil watched as the plane's landing wheels hit an electric wire. The plane smashed into the ground.

The other boys stood and stared. *Would the plane explode?* they wondered.

Neil didn't hesitate. He sprinted to the

plane. He was determined to rescue the pilot and his student.

Neil helped the flight instructor out of the plane. He was shaken up but not hurt. Neil looked at the student taking lessons. Neil gently eased the boy out of his seat. Then Neil recognized the badly injured boy. He was Neil's friend and classmate Chuck Finken-bine!

Neil held Chuck's battered body in his arms as his friend died.

Neil could hardly talk to his parents or friends for the next few days. After school he just went to his room to think about his friend and to think about flying.

Neil reached a decision. He knew flying was dangerous — Chuck's death had shown him that. But Neil also knew he simply could not stop flying. Flying was part of who Neil Armstrong was. Neil made up his mind to become the best and safest pilot he possibly could be. With that goal in mind, Neil stud-ied flying twice as hard as ever before.

Neil studied so hard that he was able to graduate from high school in the spring of 1947. Neil was young but ready to move on with his life. Under his picture in the school yearbook a friend wrote, *He Thinks. He Acts, T'is Done*. Neil's friend understood that when Neil made up his mind to do something, he did it!

One fall evening, Neil was talking with Mr. John Crites, his math and science teacher in junior high. Neil was sharing his hopes and dreams. As Neil and Mr. Crites gazed at the huge harvest moon rising, Neil said, "Someday I want to go to that moon."

Mr. Crites smiled and said nothing. What was there to say? Going to the moon was an impossible dream even for a student as smart and talented as Neil Armstrong was.

But Neil was determined to take steps to make his dream come true. Neil decided to go to college to become an airplane engineer. He knew his parents couldn't afford to pay for college for himself, his sister, and his brother. So Neil decided to join the Navy.

Neil agreed to fly in the Navy as a fighter pilot when he was needed. The Navy agreed to pay for Neil's college education.

Neil hadn't told his parents about his plans. But he knew he had to. He knew they might be upset because Neil might have to fly in a war. World War II had ended two years earlier. The Armstrongs knew many young men who had died in that war. In 1947 it looked like the United States might soon be fighting Russia.

One summer afternoon in 1947, Neil sat down at the kitchen table. His mother had just finished making his favorite apple dumplings. Neil silently snacked on the dumplings as his mother continued making peach jam.

All at once Neil stood up and said, "Mom, I've joined the Navy, and I'm going to be a fighter pilot."

Mrs. Armstrong was so surprised that she dropped a large jar of jam. The jar landed on her big toe and exploded. Mrs. Armstrong was covered from head to toe with peach jam. She was hopping up and down because

her toe was broken, too. Neil rushed to help his mother, but he slipped in the peach jam. Then Mr. Armstrong walked in to see what the commotion was all about. He stood speechless, staring at his hopping, crying wife and his son seated on the floor in peach jam.

Mr. Armstrong and Neil took Mrs. Armstrong to the doctor. He bandaged her broken toe. Mrs. Armstrong, however, was more worried about Neil than her toe. His news meant he might have to fight in the next war, if there was one. Mrs. Armstrong sadly said, "My foot hurt like crazy, but the real pain was in my heart."

9
Neil Fights and Flies

In September 1947 Neil began college at Purdue University, in Indiana. He had picked Purdue because it was only 150 miles from home. Best of all, Purdue was one of the top engineering colleges in the country. Neil continued to follow his dream of learning how to design real airplanes.

Neil took every math, science, and aviation class he could. He worked to complete his Eagle Scout rank, the highest in scouting. He drilled with other Navy cadets and studied seamanship. He joined the American Rocket Society. He became a member of the Aero Club. Neil especially enjoyed this club because everyone in it had the same passion for flying. The young men built model airplanes with tiny motors and propellers. Neil flew his planes outside in good weather. When the weather was bad Neil got up early and flew his models in a large auditorium. He even had a job delivering the local newspaper in the morning before classes began.

Neil read in the newspaper about the war the United States was beginning to fight in Korea. He wondered when the Navy would call him up to join the fight.

That call came in January 1949. Neil was ordered to report for flight training in Florida. He knew flying in combat would be dangerous, but Neil was also excited. Now he would be able to fly jets and become an even better pilot.

Neil Armstrong was nineteen years old when he began flying Navy planes. Neil did so well that he was sent for advanced pilot training. Neil learned how to take off and land his jet on an aircraft carrier in the sea. After a year of training, Neil was ready to fly combat missions. Neil was sent to San Diego to join the flying crew aboard the

U.S.S. *Essex*. On July 5, 1951, the *Essex* sailed to Korea. The *Essex* was going to be Neil's home for many long months.

As usual, Neil found ways to keep busy during the weeks at sea. He taught math classes for sailors. He chatted with the mechanics taking care of the planes to help them better understand their jobs. Anyone who wanted to learn something new went to Neil for help.

When the *Essex* reached Korea, Neil began flying combat missions. He bombed bridges. He shot at military targets. Neil attacked enemy supply lines. Each flight meant taking off from his ship that was moving in the ocean. He had to land back on the ship's deck in good weather, bad weather, even at night.

Before long, Neil Armstrong had the reputation of being an excellent pilot.

But the flying was very dangerous. The enemy soldiers shot at the American planes. Some of the planes were shot down. Others crashed in accidents. Neil was sad when any of his fellow flyers didn't return.

One day, Neil almost didn't return, either. His plane was hit by enemy gunfire. Neil's plane could barely fly, and he was only twenty feet off the ground! Neil did everything he had learned to do in the event of an accident. He dropped his cannons. He dumped extra fuel. Slowly and patiently, the plane gained altitude. But he knew his damaged plane could not fly back to the *Essex*. He would have to bail out.

Neil decided to keep his plane flying as long as he could. He hoped to get out of enemy territory before bailing out. Finally, Neil was out of enemy territory, but his plane was almost ready to crash. Neil threw out anything that might hurt him when he ejected. His flying helmet was the last thing he tossed out.

Neil pushed the ejection seat button. The seat sent Neil out of the plane and into the air. But he was spinning out of control! Neil fell four thousand feet before he could get into the right position to open his parachute. He yanked on the parachute ripcord. The huge yellow parachute popped open, but not all the way! Neil was spinning like a top! Calmly thinking through the situation, Neil realized he could stop the spinning by pulling on the parachute cords. Neil pulled at the cords, stopped the spinning, and safely landed in a rice paddy.

Then he saw a Korean man hurrying toward him. Neil thought the man might be an enemy soldier. Instead, the man had come to give Neil's helmet back! The helmet had fallen ten thousand feet and almost hit the Korean man.

When he was safely back on board his ship, the other flyers teased Neil. They told him he would have to pay because he damaged his helmet.

Neil had other near misses on his flights. But he always stayed calm, thought through the problem, found a solution, and returned safely each time. Neil flew seventy-eight missions and received five medals for his bravery.

10
That's One Small Step for Man, One Giant Leap for Mankind

After three years in the Navy, Neil returned to Purdue. He finished his engineering degree in January 1955. He got a job that suited him perfectly. He became a test pilot and flight engineer for the group that was developing the space program. Neil was able to combine his three passions: flying, engineering, and space.

Neil's work took him to California, where he tested the fastest, highest-flying planes in the world. He pushed the planes to their limits. He pushed himself hard, too. As usual, Neil wanted to be the best at what he did. Neil's reputation as an excellent pilot grew.

He was also becoming well known for his engineering insights into improving jets.

In 1956 Neil married Janet Shearon. The Armstrongs had three children: Ricky, Karen, and Mark. Sadly, Karen died from a brain tumor when she was only two years old.

In 1962 the National Aeronautics and Space Administration (NASA) began looking for a second group of astronauts. Neil applied for the astronaut program. Two hundred fifty-three pilots hoped to be astronauts. Only nine were selected, and Neil Armstrong was one of them!

The Armstrong family moved to Houston, Texas, where the astronauts were trained. Neil learned how to steer a spacecraft. He learned how to work in space without any gravity. He was assigned the job to help engineer test simulators, which trained astronauts to fly a spaceship without leaving Earth.

Neil's first trip into space came in 1966. Neil blasted off on March 16, 1966, aboard *Gemini 8*. He stayed in orbit around Earth for three days. Neil was in command of the flight. The crew's mission was to dock the space capsule with a satellite. No one had ever done this before. Before flying to the moon could be successfully accomplished, it was necessary to bring two spacecraft together. Using his flying skills, Neil gently docked his capsule with the satellite. Neil said to flight control in Houston, "Flight, we are docked! It's really a smoothie."

With this docking success, Neil was one step closer to going to the moon. Then suddenly, the two spacecraft began spinning out of control. Neil released the satellite but the spinning got even worse. Neil and his crew were spinning so fast they almost blacked out. But Neil solved the problem and brought *Gemini 8* safely back to Earth.

Neil was assigned to the *Apollo* program. Its mission was to land a man on the moon in 1969. No one knew who would be chosen to be the first person to set foot on the moon. Like the other *Apollo* astronauts, Neil hoped he might be the one.

Neil trained for the moon mission. He

practiced flying and landing the spacecraft that would land on the moon. One time, when Neil was flying the machine, it exploded in the air. Neil bailed out and landed safely.

On January 6, 1969, Neil was told that he would be the commander of *Apollo 11*. It was going to make the first landing on the moon! Edward "Buzz" Aldrin and Michael Collins would join Neil Armstrong on this historic mission.

When asked how he felt, Neil explained that he just wanted his mission to be safe. He said, "What I really want to be, in all honesty, is the first man back from the moon."

On July 16, 1969, *Apollo 11* was ready. At 9:32 A.M. the rocket blasted off from Cape Kennedy. More than a million people gathered nearby to watch the liftoff. Millions more watched on television.

Neil Armstrong was finally on his way to the moon! It took Neil, Buzz, and Michael three days to reach the moon in *Columbia,* their space capsule. *Eagle*, the lunar lander, was attached to *Columbia*.

On July 19, *Columbia* orbited the moon. Neil and Buzz climbed into the tiny *Eagle*. They undocked from *Columbia* and began dropping toward the moon.

Neil was commanding *Eagle*. The computers on board were guiding *Eagle* to its landing place on the moon. When they were close, Neil looked out the window. He saw dozens of huge boulders. They couldn't land there! So Neil took control of *Eagle* himself.

Slowly, he guided *Eagle*. But *Eagle's* landing rockets were running out of fuel! Neil searched for a place to land. Finally, he saw one. Neil gently guided *Eagle* onto the moon. He had only sixteen seconds of fuel left before *Eagle* would have crashed.

Then Neil Armstrong said these famous words, "The *Eagle* has landed."

For the first time in history, people had landed safely on the moon.

Neil and Buzz ate and rested before their next big project, walking on the moon. NASA had picked Neil to be the first man on the moon. Buzz Aldrin would be second. Both

astronauts put on their special space suits. Neil opened *Eagle*'s door.

Neil slowly climbed down the ladder. He stopped at the bottom to look around. Back on Earth, millions of people were watching Neil.

Then Neil Armstrong stepped into history. He put his left foot down on the moon!

Neil said, "That's one small step for man, one giant leap for mankind."

Neil Armstrong's dream had come true. He had stepped on the moon. And he was the first person to have ever done so.

Neil took more steps, leaving the first human footprints on the moon. And because the moon has no wind or rain, Neil Armstrong's footprints will remain on the moon for millions of years.

Who would have guessed, on the hot August day in 1930 when Stephen and Viola Armstrong first looked at their son Neil's tiny feet, that his feet would take such important steps?